WANDERS WONDERS

design for a New Age

Het Kruithuis, Museum of Contemporary Art, 's-Hertogenbosch

010 Publishers, Rotterdam

Contents

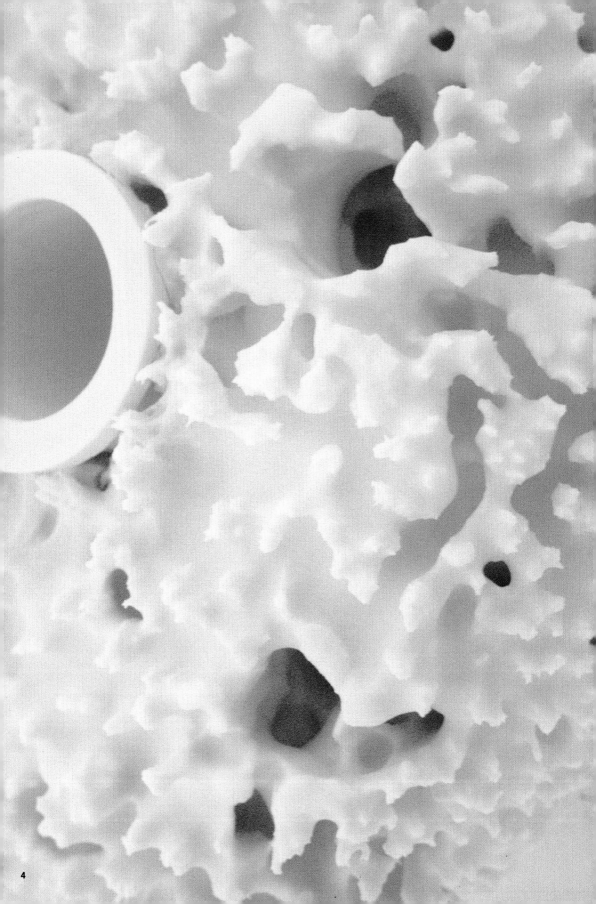

The 20th century may go down in history as a period of discoveries, inventions and renewal - taking the positive view, that is. People's lives have grown much more comfortable over the past hundred years, thanks to revolutions both large and small in the fields of technology, material use and production methods. In many cases, however, new advances no longer have the time to grow old before they themselves are superseded by something newer still. Familiarity breeds contempt and so we rush from one novelty to the next. Abundance allows us to forget with a clear conscience, as it is no longer in our power to remember everything.
What is so wonderful about the designs of Marcel Wanders and his associates is that remembering and familiarity are such an important part of their newness. And the way the profundity of their design philosophy invariably translates into such clear and bright products. Wanders' designs are encapsulated in these resonant paradoxes. They generate a certain sensation and the shock of recognition.

Wanders Wonders is not about inventing the wheel but about the wheel of invention.

Yvònne G.J.M. Joris
Director Het Kruithuis, Museum of Contemporary Art

Designers think up pleasing, beautiful or amusing forms. They have a feeling for colour and style and boundless imagination. It is thanks to their creativity that we can always buy 'something new' - the image that invariably confronts us in our magazines. The stream of chairs, tables, lamps, plates and so on that has sprung over the years from the creative brains of our designers has reached dizzying proportions. It seems unstoppable - more, more and more again, year after year.

And still there has to be something new.

What's more, designers once thought they could make the world a better place with their work. Full of idealism, they told us great stories about the beneficial influence of their designs, about an aesthetically justifiable mass production, about good and attractive things for all and about the uplifting of humanity. Little did they suspect that humanity preferred to go its own way, leaving them shut up in their ivory towers.

Engagement has become a rare commodity now that the great emancipatory narratives have fallen silent and designers have become individualistic and realistic. Our age is one of total relativism. We lack a common purpose. Design has become a practice without content, geared towards surface appearance and financial success.

Nevertheless, from time to time, you still come across designers who are concerned about their craft. While fulfilling their professional duty to design new products, a nagging feeling takes hold of them that they are not really serving society. They're not, after all, in a position to solve the great social and ecological issues of our time. All they can do is to add yet another product to the current surfeit, when those that exist already have so much to offer. And not everyone feels the call to create water-pumps or utility vehicles for local people in Africa, to design wheelchairs and other useful devices or to conceive environmentally-friendly products on the basis of detailed lifecycle analyses.

Many designers chose the profession because of a personal drive and the urge to create. That does not, however, preclude a sense of engagement. The great emancipatory narratives have gone: now it is the turn of small stories, rooted in everyday reality. Stories that tell of products capable of ageing gracefully and allowing the user to bond with them, of the value of the things that already exist, of personal ecology, of uncertainty, dreams, passion and pleasure. These are not moralising tales, nor do they proclaim any universal truths. But they dare to put forward different truths and even to sound paradoxical. They are small stories that everyone can understand, stories that are well worth retelling. They will not radically change the world, but they do give meaning to our culture. Thanks to them, we will not only find superficial acquaintances within the endless stream of new products, we may also make one or two friends for life.

Renny Ramakers

Marcel Wanders works the 'Wonders' of his firm's name mainly through impregnation. He infuses knotted string with epoxy to make a chair, pours clay around a sponge to create a vase, and uses condoms as moulds for vases. More than that, he infuses the unformed and the unarticulated with meaning. What was amorphous takes shape without gaining weight. Out of the flows of plastics and resins that so closely trace the fast flows of capital that mould our world, Wanders makes moments of form.

As such, Wanders' designs are a continuation of some of the central concerns of canonical modernist design. They abstract type, create mass-producable versions of ancient objects, marry use and ideal, and make use of the most modern materials. They manage to avoid, however, the split between ideal form and vernacular bricolage that runs like a fissure through most of the design production of this century. By going with the flow, Wanders has continued a crucial concern to all those who have sought to represent the continual changes wrought by the technologies that continually remake our world.

We live in an age of steel, speed and plastic. If the Cubists and the Futurists believed that they could represent the shape of change itself by exposing the many facets of a reality that we could not stop and understand from one standpoint, then more practical designers picked up on the essential building blocks of this new world, which were almost all malleable crystallisations of chemical assemblages. Almost all the objects in our world are artificial. Steel and later aluminium formed themselves out of molten ore infused with chemicals. Bakelite and plastic are products of oil that can create infinitely flexible facsimiles of anything around us. Fluidity has only increased in the period since the computer has broken all reality down into malleable bytes: with the aid of CADD, Photoshop and every other visualisation and animation program, and computer-aided milling, we can now imagine, display and then mill almost any shape we want. Reality is truly fluid.

The plasticity of our environment is essential. Any art work that would not be a nostalgic recreation of the past must be a representative and representational part of this world. The question remains: if all is flow, what is real? What is the shape of this river of forms that inundates us every day? To many designers, any object must be no more and no less than the solid version of flow. It must be a 'blob': the result of the sculpting of material not by intuition, but out of the integrative logic of technology (the computer program, most often) itself. To others, the ability to create endlessly perfect copies without an original in continuous variations means that an object must either be as abstract as possible or a whimsical joke that makes its point and is then recycled. Between Karim Rashid and Philippe Starck, between Marc Newson and Jasper Morrison, a world of high-design objects is spreading its veneer of good taste and perceptive interpretation over the diurnal flows.

Wanders shares some interests with these designers. His Breakfast for a Dwarf Rabbit necklace is as witty as anything Starck has produced, while his vases evoke both ancient prototypes and the asymmetrical variations that turn up in so many design shops today. Where Wanders distinguished himself is in the making of objects that escape from the fluidity of funniness and slick form by presenting themselves as frozen monuments. His famous Set Up Shades work with the endless serial production of identical objects that have been streamlined by taste and for ease of manufacturing to create something whose very seriality makes it stand out from its context. His Lace Table turns a perfectly white modernist cube into a piece of furniture that is strange not because of its abstraction, but because it is both porous and evocative of an old piece of lace one would drape around the shoulder, here turned into a hardened relic.

The context for such work is, to a certain extent, the Netherlands. The Dutch ability to adopt modernist traditions with a minimum of fuss, a touch of irony, and a healthy disregard for convention has liberated Wanders and many of his compatriots to produce some of the wryest pieces of industrial design currently on the market. Add into this no-nonsense attitude the Dutch respect for an environment they have manipulated endlessly to let them survive, but which they realise is fragile and always might take its revenge, and you get a design climate in which the making of simple, recyclable objects that make us aware, above all else, of the artificiality of our work, can flourish.

In this artificial garden, Wanders creates some of the most beautiful, if not the brightest, flowers. They are not at all reminiscent of traditional Dutch forms, as are the designs of several of his erstwhile colleagues in the Droog co-operative (though he does acknowledge the work of the great glass designer Andries Copier in some of his work). Yet they do not disappear seamlessly into an international context either. Instead, they are highly specific in their invention. Wanders is a well-trained industrial designer who knows how to attack problems like how to make a credit card holder that really works (Card Case), or who can make recyclable glasses for an airline that keep hot and cold beverages manageable (Glasses for British Airways). He also knows how to make elegant objects.

Where things become interesting is where Wanders does not so much break the rules in which he was trained, as elaborate them. The epoxy chair hovers in its imagery between Danish modern and thrift-store Third World, between old-fashioned ease and modern poise. It is a piece of handicraft that is slightly disturbing because of its texture and lack of weight. It appears more like a ghost than a real thing. The Stack Up Shades have the same effect. They are familiar, but not quite logical. Something about them is not quite normal, not quite real.

This is what Wanders' Wonders achieve: they make us wonder. As we go swimming from form to form, as our factories and computers go on spewing out image after image, Wanders creates a stutter, a frieze in the flows, a freeze frame. For a moment, we stop, try to figure out what haunts us, how the object works, what it is made out of, why it looks the way it does. We might then continue in our frenetic movements, but Wanders' spare moments will continue to remind us that somewhere and somehow we must stop, make, use, reflect. If architecture is frozen music, then Wanders' designs are the ice cubes of the fast flows of modern capital and the artificial landscape it creates.

Aaron Betsky

The work of Marcel Wanders is placed within that range of researches that investigate about a new relationship between technology and nature. Since a long time these two areas have been considered in conflict and alternative: where technology came, nature disappeared, as well as the contrary.

Today finally design finds out that this conflict can be by-passed: technology has become a second friendly nature, that surrounds us, and sets with us a complex and flexible interface.

On the other hand, nature can be considered a quite advanced technology, a deep energy of transformation of the world.

Andrea Branzi

...The supermarket lights gleamed against the dull grey winter sky. Marcel did not forget to buy a few eggs to cook up his new vase. 'Time to go home' he thought as he approached the counter, 'and finish knotting the chair'. Marcel's is a hard-lace world...

Marcel Wanders belongs to a very contemporary group of designers whose elective mission is to endow objects with a communicative soul. In their universe, things are no longer what they seem, but rather what they say without speaking. Sitting in the Knotted Chair is an experience that is bound to elicit very personal memories and associations - Grandma's crochet, a hammock in the big magnolia tree in the old country house, hours and hours of knots back at the sailing school - a function that is not normally required of a chair. Similarly, Wanders shapes solid lace in parallelepipeds to form little tables, but the form of a table seems just a pretext. In a way, so is its function. What matters is the ability of the object to evoke feeling and meaning.

Curiously, the way to reach this transcendental state is by diving into the most physical world of materials and techniques. Some Dutch designers, and Marcel in particular, have been the first to manifest a new balance between technology and artefacts that is a crucial contemporary ideal. All over the world, designers are not glorifying advanced technology in the way they did during the high-tech 1980s. Rather, they are exploiting it for its ability to build not only our visual and material landscape, but also our emotional and psychological one.

Learning through experience and manipulation, lulling his own passion and obsession until they became powerful creative tools, Wanders has created in his objects connections that were as unexpected as they were revealing. In his light and surprising objects, the poetry of the individual design process is displayed in a straightforward and honest fashion, albeit with complex technique. Good design is still a timeless concept, best exemplified by an object that works efficiently for its purposes, is manufactured soundly, contains suggestions that go beyond its form and function, and is beautiful. Wanders' technological impressionism represents the last frontier of modern design.

Paola Antonelli

Wanders Wonders. He Wanders. He Wonders.
Wanders Wonders. He does.
Wanders Wonders. They are.

Writing about the work of Marcel Wanders somehow makes you want to try to do the same, apparently simple things he does in his best designs. These consist of smaller or larger variations on existing things and ways of manufacturing that suddenly make you realise how much beauty, power and potential they actually conceal. They may be simple things that we have all seen and used before, yet Wanders can still make us wonder about them.

There is a rare lightness about Wanders' work. Ask a writer, a filmmaker or a musician and he or she will tell you that the most difficult thing on earth is to produce a light piece. Before you know it, the result becomes superficial or sentimental, or loses its tension. That never happens with Wanders. Even though his work generally looks simple and relaxed - as if he thought it up on a Sunday morning - there is always a hint of dadaism or surrealism. His experiments with lampshades remind me of Man Ray's 'Obstruction' mobile (1920), made of coat-hangers. Wanders himself says that he is not so much interested in the ready-made aspect, but in reusing the archetype. The archetypal lampshade is, indeed, worth reviving, given what it has become in the past five or ten years, simply because it produces a pleasant light. But one or two would have made the point. Wanders' stackings, multiplications and enlargements turn them into something more than simple lampshades. It is not merely a question of having more of a good thing - the repetitions and changes make you wonder about <u>the</u> archetypal lampshade.

Wanders asks in one of his articles how we expect beauty to spring from a container that has first been filled with garbage. His question - largely rhetorical - puts me in mind of the French artist, Hubert Duprat, one of whose works consists of small aquariums in which he keeps caddis-flies. These normally produce small, fragile cylinders of sand and saliva in which to live. Duprat, however, put them in an environment comprising flakes of gold and tiny jewels, which the flies turned into the most beautiful and delicate homes imaginable. He videoed them at work. Removed from the aquarium - how cruel - the flies' houses look like brooches. The ordinary cylinders and the fancy ones are, to my mind, equally beautiful - it depends on what you do with them. Through this work, Duprat successfully brought out the qualities that give nature the power to surprise us. In other works, he uses coral and bread dough or wooden branches, covered with ivory, that grow together in an unexpected way - the 'how' remains invisible. Duprat does not appear to be interested in the ready-made either, but in the 'already-there'. He insists on the 'sideration effect' that the real has upon him)

Wanders comes very close to Duprat and his caddis-flies. From completely ordinary materials - eggs, condoms, sponges - he creates the most serene and delicate objects. His saliva is more high-tech, though, even if that is not immediately obvious. When he does use precious, delicate and decorative materials like lace or macramé, he reveals a desire to turn them into something normal, something rigid and tough, that you can actually use and not just look at. Take his Knotted Chair and Lace Tables, which Meret Oppenheim is sure to have liked.

I understand now why Louis Armstrong always seemed to me to sing about a 'wanderful' rather than a 'wonderful' world.

Bart Lootsma

Marcel Wanders

INTRODUCTION

Since I've been involved in developing products and ideas, a number of questions
I couldn't answer and dreams I wanted to make real have played an essential part
in my life.

As a designer, I felt powerless in the face of a range of ecological issues. In the
first place, the useful life of products is getting shorter and shorter. Products are
increasingly unable to retain their quality, they rarely satisfy our real needs and
they lack any kind of 'soul-mate' quality. That robs them of the opportunity to
grow old gracefully and they are prematurely replaced. Then there is the fact that
every innovation demands another, creating a throwaway culture in which more
and more energy and materials are used to less and less effect. I didn't know how,
with this desire for new products, I would be able to combine my need to live in
and contribute to a healthy environment. I also dreamed, finally, about products
that not only offered more quality but could also bring together a variety of
qualities. Products that would be complete and hence genuinely significant to the
user. Objects that touch you and that generate a positive feeling. In short:
products worth bonding with for a lifetime.

Finding answers was infinitely important if I was to retain my belief in design.
This quest gave rise to a number of interesting possibilities: not laws, rules or
absolute truths, but concepts I would like to share in the hope that they become
as important to you as they are to me.

I'd like to thank Inez van der Linden for her immense contribution to this book.
She has managed to draw the essential out of my words and notes and to translate
them into concise and informative pieces of text.

Marcel Wanders

'Here to create an environment of love, to live with passion and to make my most
exciting dreams come true'

There is no certainty about the things around us. It is up to our creativity to raise this uncertainty to the level of poetry.

DESIGNER OF MEANING

Life to me is fabulous. It offers so many surprises - the warmest people, the most compelling sounds and the most beautiful shapes. All these experiences mean that I am alive. They make me a part of the world and enable me to know who I am.
I know that these things influence me, but I have also discovered that I am the one who creates them.
I think I can only change my world by renewing my thoughts, by casting doubt on certainties, by mobilising what is static and by asking myself what all the things around me really mean.
The senses do not provide access to absolute truth. Experiences only take on meaning through personal memories, personal belief structures and personal choices. My environment is not what I see, hear, feel, smell or taste: it is what I decide I want to see, hear, feel, smell or taste. And even then, I am the one who gives meaning to it all. I am the scriptwriter of my world. I give reason and meaning to that world and everything that happens within it. In giving that meaning, I create my world.
This possibility is not the exclusive preserve of designers. Whether you like it or not, everyone is responsible for creating their own world. The only difference between designer and user is that the designer has made a career of creating meaning. Designers specialise in renewing the meaning of everything around them by creating new shapes, ideas, functions, combinations, habits and stories - by renewing the message.

Nothing has meaning but the meaning you give it.

Nomad carpet, Wanders Wonders for Cappellini.
One side of the carpet can be raised to form a comfortable
back support, turning the carpet into a simple seat.

Tamagotchi, Aki Maita for Bandai.
The arrival of the Tamagotchi totally transformed the idea of children's toys.
The game lasts for weeks instead of minutes.
The electronic pet lives longer the better it's cared for, but it always returns
to its home planet eventually.

Live a congruent lifestyle, in which you find a balance between seemingly contradictory wishes. Live a life that is not only good for others, but also for you. I try to create ecology-supporting qualities and challenge people again and again to pursue their own personal ecology and development. This concerns my products (the target) as well as my organisation (the path).

PERSONAL ECOLOGY

In my view, it is absolutely impossible to think about a better world ecology without recognising that it starts with me. You can't expect people to respect the world if they do not respect themselves and do not take care of their health, their dreams and their passions. So long as I don't respect my own life, it is difficult to respect the world I live in.

This, to me, is a perfect point of departure for design - conceiving products and ideas that help people to discover a 'healthier' lifestyle. In other words, a lifestyle that allows space for consciousness and for wider, greater and universal respect. The only way to achieve these products is to live honestly and respectfully and to design ecologically. I call this 'personal ecology'. Personal ecology is about the way I think about others and myself. About how I realise my dreams, take myself seriously and am honest with myself. It is about what I find to be good and bad, and about going with those feelings. The process is a continuing and everlasting one. The implications of personal ecology are that I have no option but to create respectful products and ideas that contribute positively to my surroundings. Designing products with no such respect occurs at the expense of my personal ecology.

As a designer, I have the ultimate opportunity to create the most fantastic ideas and objects and hence to translate my personal ecology to my surroundings and the people in them.

How can you expect beauty to spring from a container that you have first filled with garbage?

Tulips, Wanders Wonders, prototype.
This french-fry substitute is made from biodynamic rice, maize and herbs and is cooked in a transparent, fat-free Arfa oven.

Baby Jogger, The Baby Jogger Company.
The baby jogger allows two important activities to be combined, promoting a personal ecology.

A product is nothing more or less than a collection of information that has to be nurtured when developing a new product in order to achieve the greatest possible quality.

DESIGNER OF INFORMATION

I find it fascinating to consider products as collections of information, as this is the ultimate form in which they are communicated. Human beings understand the things around them by gathering information about them and then coming to a conclusion. A dog, for instance, is a mixture of a hairy garment, a bouncing ball and a baby sticking out its tongue. In this way, people create an image through which they can understand their environment. It is information about what our surroundings are and it tells us whether we will feel connected to it or will struggle against it. We can see and understand even the purely physical appearance of our surroundings only by making links with information we have accumulated in the past. In other words, understanding is based on knowledge of underlying aspects and prior experience.

If a product is understood as information, it should also be designed that way. If I were only to express myself in tangible form, I would not only be selling myself short, I would also be taking the long way around. I ought to develop into an information-maker with many more creative means at my disposal than form alone, and who can use them to expand the significance of things. It all comes down, of course, to the quality of the information.

Egg Vase, Wanders Wonders for Droog Design, Cappellini.
The prototype of the egg vase was created by filling condoms with hard-boiled eggs.

Access Swatch, Swatch.
The Access Swatch has a quartz movement and a chip that gives
the wearer access to particular events. One has already been
produced for all the main museums in Rome, and another for all
the matches played by Juventus.
It can also be loaded for ski-slope access.

Musicall Swatch, Swatch.
The Musicall Swatch has an alarm function with sounds by
famous contemporary composers like Jean Michel Jarre,
Robert Palmer and Candy Dulfer.

Durability in the field of ideas, relationships, objects, and so on, not only to create a world that is less wasteful but also to create deeper and more meaningful relationships with our environment.

BABY-FACE FIXATION

Our culture lacks respect for the old. Once I recognised this, I found myself confronted with it constantly. We prefer the new to the old. New things are considered better, old news is no news. Products have to be smooth, taut and flawless. Sadly, it appears that this fixation on the new and the young is even stronger among designers than other people. I suspect that they (including myself) have even less respect than others for the old, as it is their profession to create new things. We suffer from what I call 'baby-face fixation'.

There is, of course, nothing wrong with appreciating the young, providing it is not at the expense of the old. Baby-face fixation leads, however, to products with few if any old metaphors: they look like eggs, babies, young girls and manga heroes. 'Young' products of this kind do not get the chance to grow old gracefully - they are precluded from the outset from any possibility of gaining character in the course of their useful life. The first scratch, a hipper version, a new fashion or a new idea immediately destroys its 'new quality'. The upshot is replacement or disposal, even though under other circumstances, a scratch or a hipper model could have enabled the product to develop its own patina and to gain character. The new character could tie in with the other old metaphors in the product.

The life expectancy of baby-face designs is very short. This makes them temporary friends on which users cannot truly rely and which will never become a real part of their lives. Baby-face fixation is a problem in a world in which lasting quality and a unique bond between product and user is important.

Since I would like many of my products to enter into a long-term relationship with the user, I use both old and new metaphors in the materials and material expressions that I apply. By using old metaphors in my products, I communicate a respect for old age in general. This leads to a more respectful, more acceptable and more natural ageing of my products (age with dignity). These products have the possibility of gaining quality during their life, they are more durable and it is possible to have a long-lasting relationship with them.

Lace Table, Wanders Wonders, prototype.

Roof Sogo, Frank Gehry, Barcelona.
Weaving this form in metal produced a strong and durable image.

I have a lot of respect for the new, but even more for what exists already. That's why I prefer to work within the boundaries of what is 'natural' and unforced.

ARCHETYPES

According to the British biologist Rupert Sheldrake, there are no fixed laws in the universe, merely habits and tendencies. Events, Sheldrake argues, do not occur in a specific way because of some immutable law but because similar things happened that way in the past and left a certain impression. Since the beginning of human civilisation, those impressions have created all manner of fields. Energy fields like joy, success and earth, plus all kinds of projections of objects have their place. This is also the place of the natural form, the ultimate archetype of things and ideas. I mostly work in that area because I feel the need to make products that relate to existing things, things that may seem at first sight to be familiar friends. This need arose from my great respect for what already exists. Products also complement existing energy fields. Producing in large editions, which is inherent to industrial design, represents the multiplication of an object's influence. I consider that to be a responsibility.

Set-up Shades, Wanders Wonders for Droog Design, DMD.

Table Blanche, Ann Demeulemeester for Bulo.

Horizontal: technical, material, objective, masculine, functional, conceptual, intellectual, head.
Vertical: intuitive, spiritual, stylistic, feminine, between heaven and earth, instinctive, heart.
The total information of a product can be mainly horizontal or mainly vertical. Real quality only exists where these two intersect.

HORIZONTAL/VERTICAL

According to Thorwald Detlefsen's book Esoteric Psychology, it is possible to understand the world by looking at the links that exist between and within the things in our environment. He distinguishes between horizontal and vertical. Horizontal links consist of functional, analysable and conceptual links - relationships in terms of materials, measurements, performance, and so on. Relationships of this kind are generally recognised as objective and truthful. In addition to horizontal links, there are also vertical ones - relationships in terms of character and style, between heaven and earth. These are subjective relationships located in the unconscious, which can be sensed but are difficult to prove.

It is clear to me that the best designs have both horizontal and vertical links. Many products, by contrast are designed in a largely horizontal/objective or vertical/subjective way. In the case of 'objective' products, I know, for instance, what they can do and I know their value, but they simply do not feel good. On the other hand, there are 'subjective' products which feel right and cheer me up from the first sight, but which do not tell me what use they are to me or what I ought to do with them.

Fortunately, most products are located somewhere between these two extremes, but very few are located at that point of intersection where true quality lies. These are the objects that give me a good feeling, which I can relate to, which are beautiful, but which are also logical and intelligent, which tell a story I want to hear and make me feel intelligent.

Because I respect both horizontally and vertically oriented people, I work at the intersection of both. I set out to touch as large a group of people as possible with as complete as possible a product.

There is a striking parallel between the division of horizontal and vertical and that between typical industrial product design and product styling.
Outer beauty relies on inner beauty, which, according to the Hindu doctrine of Ayurveda arises 'spontaneously' when an individual accepts him or herself and when body and mind are harmoniously balanced.

Sponge Vase, Wanders Wonders for Droog Design, Cappellini.
The sponge vase was made by dipping a sponge in clay and firing it.
In the process, the clay copies the form and structure of the sponge.

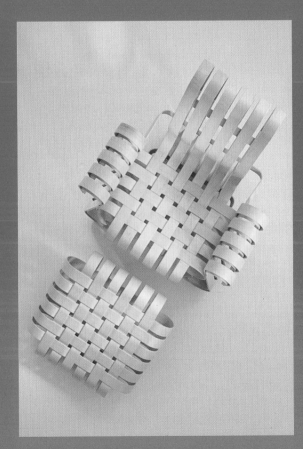

Chair, Frank Gehry for Knoll.

A good communicator 'talks' in the language of his audience. Out of respect for his audience and with the knowledge that it will enable them to understand his message. Successful communication is based on the notion of anticipating individual perception.

DESIGNER FOR SENSES

Our environment continuously confronts us with immense quantities of information that demand our attention. As a child, you learn how to focus your attention on the right things, on the things that are important to you, whether or not they are appropriate. You probably continue to do so every day. Because each person learns individually how to detect information, we all develop a personal filter system through which we pick up and transmit information. These filters correspond with our senses. The three largest groups through which people appear to gather information are the face (visual), hearing (auditory) and touch (kinaesthetic).

Every person receives information through these three channels.

A balanced individual, if such a person exists, would filter out an equal amount of information from each filter. In reality, however, people are not so finely balanced and one sense tends to dominate. Visual people largely gain their information by looking. They extract information from shapes, colours and material expression. Auditory people orient themselves primarily through hearing. They receive their information from sound, but also from objective, precise facts. Kinaesthetic people are chiefly informed by touch, both physical and emotional. Every imaginable combination between the three is, of course, possible.

This is very important to me because I want to communicate with as many people as possible through my designs. As I want my message, my story, to get across, I have to speak the right language, even if it is simply a matter of respect for those with whom I am communicating (after all, you don't greet an Italian by saying 'hello'). This means that I want to give my designs visual, auditory and kinaesthetic information in order to be interesting to a wide group. Whether it will be genuinely important to people is determined by the quality of the information.

Communication stops when the speaker stops speaking or the listener stops listening

Knotted chair, Wanders Wonders for Droog Design, Cappellini.
This chair is made from aramide and carbon rope. Each one is carefully knotted by
hand, impregnated and suspended in a frame. The ultimate shape of the chair is
determined by gravity, making every one unique.

Pop (Marco), Marco Tucolsa for Unicef.
Unicef asks schoolchildren to make a doll and offer it for adoption.
It then sells the dolls, accompanied by a letter from the maker to
the adoptive parents, asking them to write back (My daughter Joy is very happy
with Marco and is taking good care of him).

We are not looking for stylisms – the world only moves when we are able to change the meaning of our surroundings.

THE QUALITY OF INFORMATION

Honesty and truth play an important role in the history of design.
Since Bauhaus, 'production technology' or the structure of the production process, has been the principal message communicated to the end-user. This story is expressed in products through a clear structure that makes the technology visible.
There is nothing wrong with telling what is logical, honest or obvious. On the other hand, the story will often be a dull one. The creative spirit is capable of much more than this sober, limited design truth. It is time to tell a different story - one that is more interesting, inspiring and valuable, which gives a new meaning and not only matches but expands our view of the world.
I believe that designers ought to take 'honest lies' seriously, as it offers them an opportunity to give real meaning to our environment and to exert a positive influence on the people who live in it.

'An honest lie is better than a boring truth'

Vase (Ming), Wanders Wonders for Cappellini.
This porcelain vase is a copy of a 3,100 year-old one on my mantelpiece at home.
The original vase has lots of marvellous details that recall its history.
They are supplemented in the copy with new details to create an unusual blend.

Bear Hubcaps, Ronal.
Turn your car into a cuddly toy.

It is never form that directs the development of culture. The meaning of our environment can also be changed without physical intervention.

IMMATERIAL DESIGNER

Not only can I give a product a new meaning, I can also give it several truths at once, subject of course to its physical form. I don't need form in order to change meaning - it is never form that directs the development of culture. That means I am no longer dependent on material, but merely re-order what exists already. This still gives rise to movement and a sense of the new and up-to-date, without addressing materials. That this generates uncertainty as to the being and meaning of the image is, in my view, both inevitable and a source of creativity.

My need to give meaning to culture is greater than my wish to package it in opaque disguises. In an age when the pressure on physical resources is intensifying all the time, it is up to designers to come with concepts that address the nature of our relationship with those resources. Materials will become less and less of an issue. Matter was once considered the wings of thought, to which it lent content and vision. However, the free and more rarefied thought I foresee does not require new wings; it can travel on the wind, unforced, uncultivated and natural. The wind will carry it on its way without the ballast of wings. I no longer need to drag form along behind my vanity.

When materials are scarce, thought can be the active creator of the future. Thought, living in symbiosis with existing, passive matter, will expand the quality of our information age. Thought is strong enough to carry, nimble enough to survive and immaterial enough to be reordered. The artist will become the typesetter of our culture. By reordering the existing time and time again, he or she will write poetry.

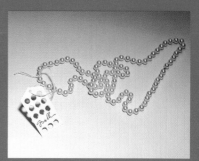

Pearl necklace, traditional pearl necklace knotted by design celebrity Gijs Bakker. Design Marcel Wanders and Dinie Besems.

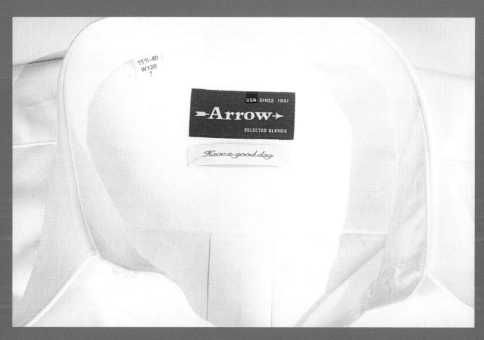

Shirt, Arrow

For us it is an absolute certainty that all our clients are served by products that are good for themselves as wel as for the bigger whole and that there is always a solution that makes this synergy possible.

FORM FOLLOWS THE GOOD

This latter idea is simple but crucially important. Acting on effective principles can seem hard, as you have to deal with clients, production schedules and a whole series of supposed reasons why it won't work. Perhaps adopting so many principles creates an extra problem, but for me it actually became plain that a whole range of factors were no longer important and the situation became easier. If, using my principles, I create a creative plan that is not only good for me and for the whole, but also has quality for my client, those principles are judged to be realistic and inspiring. I work on this basis and have found that most people, when confronted with a creative plan of this kind, can see its value and find it pleasant to work on a greater meaning.

Once upon a time, when you watched Lassie, you invariably knew who was good and who was bad. Everyone was on Lassie's side - no one was against her. Nothing's actually changed. Everyone still wants to be Lassie!

Jeff (Tommy Rettig) and Lassie.

DIPSTICK small plastic stick with compressed, instant coffee at one end.
When stirred in hot water, it produces a cup of coffee, 1985

MON CHÉRI Cupboard, 1997

The gift comprised a small bottle of Dutch gin and three stainless-steel cups.
The largest is decorated with the European flag, the medium-sized one with the Dutch flag and the smallest one
with the flag of the City of Amsterdam.
Produced by Wanders Wonders, 1997

HELDSPELD (Hero Pin)
A small jewel that makes people look for the qualities they value most in people.
Produced and distributed by Wanders Wonders, 1992

EGG VASES (Droog Design for Rosenthal)
Stuffing latex condoms with hard-boiled eggs created the shape of these porcelain vases.
Produced and distributed by Cappellini, 1997

SPONGE VASE (Droog Design for Rosenthal)

A natural sponge is impregnated with liquid clay, dried and then fired in a ceramic kiln.

The sponge disappears, but its form is reproduced perfectly in the porcelain.

The result can be manufactured industrially, yet is unique every time and brings out the best from the material, 1997

FOAM BOWL (Droog Design for Rosenthal)

The process was then taken a step further to produce ceramic objects using pre-shaped foam.

The Foam Bowl was the first illustration of the immense potential of the technique.

Produced and distributed by Cappellini, 1997

KNOTTED CHAIR (Droog Design)
A rope made of aramid twisted around a carbon core is knotted into the shape of a chair.
It is then impregnated with epoxy and hung in a frame to harden.
The final shape is created by gravity.
Produced and distributed by Cappellini, 1996

COLLECTION OF FOUR MEDALS FOR THE GAY GAMES Amsterdam 1998.
The collection comprises gold, silver, bronze and participation medals.
A total of 24,500 were produced by Wanders Wonders in 1998.

ANDRIES solid steel silver plated candleholder,
after a glass by Andries Copier c. 1930
The collection also includes a candleholder after glasses
by Tapio Wirkkala, c. 1950 and Ettore Sottsass, 1990,
forming a brief history of glass design.
Produced and distributed by Cappellini, 1995

This vase is a modern copy of a 3,100 year-old, handmade Chinese vase.
It was found on the seabed in the wreck of an old Chinese junk.
The vase was used as a jelly-jar for more than 300 years.
The product's history has now taken a new turn. Wanders Wonders copied the shape and reproduced it in white porcelain.
ike the Chinese ceramist, we have left our own makers' marks in the pot (seams, the size reduction), making visible part of its history.
Produced and distributed by Cappellini, 1997

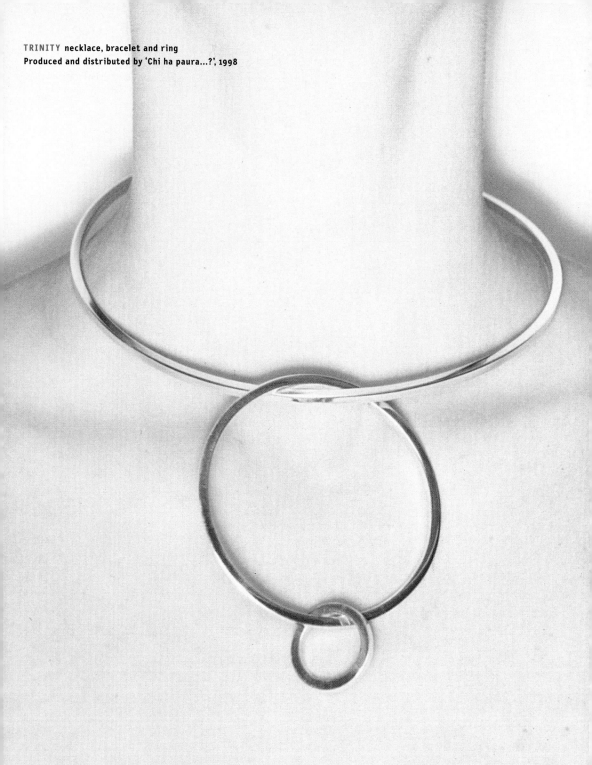

TRINITY necklace, bracelet and ring
Produced and distributed by 'Chi ha paura...?', 1998

GILDED SILVER NECKLACE, 'BREAKFAST OF A DWARF RABBIT'.
Designed in co-operation with my pet rabbit Theodore
Produced and distributed by Wanders Wonders, 1996

TAPE NECKLACE WITH THE BLISSFUL SOUND OF A RABBIT NIBBLING A CARROT
Produced and distributed by Wanders Wonders, 1996

SWING (Droog Design for Oranienbaum)
beechwood, terracotta pots, rope and ivy, 1999

ORANIENBAUMER (Droog Design for Oranienbaum)
Orange biscuits and packaging designed for production in the Oranienbaum area.
Once the biscuits have been eaten, the box can be used to grow seeds, the orange
seeds are supplied (biscuits made by the Paul Annee Bakery), 1999

APPLE JUICE BOTTLE/BIRDHOUSE
(Droog Design for Oranienbaum)
When the apple juice has been drunk and the ceramic bottle
is empty, the bottle can begin a second life as a birdhouse, 1999

BIRDHOUSE (Droog Design for Oranienbaum)
A five-star, knockdown bird restaurant, 1999

ORANIENBAUMER VIERECK (Droog Design for Oranienbaum)
Bread designed especially for bakers in the Oranienbaum area.
Each baker can produce his or her personal variation on the bread, using the standard baking tin.
There is a hole in the bread in which people can put a flower or branch to make the meal more festive
(loaf made by the Paul Annee bakery), 1999

ORANGE Dance CD (Droog Design for Oranienbaum), Music: Marcel Wanders and Ton Driessens.
All the basic sounds on this CD were recorded in the Oranienbaum area. Swans, slamming doors, raindrops, remote
control Trabbis, children and many others.
The CD contains six tracks: White Swans, Dwarfs, Snow White, Twin Drops, Angels, Nightingales. 1999.

WILLOW CHAIR **(Droog Design for Oranienbaum)**
The chair is made from unpeeled willow shoots, using traditional wickerwork techniques and shapes
(prototype made by Steffen Kolbe), 1999

The case is made from two translucent ABS shells with an ingenious folding system, in which you can keep seven
of your most precious plastic cards.
The specially designed spring-loaded closing mechanism holds the case firmly open or closed.
Produced and distributed by Wanders Wonders, 1994

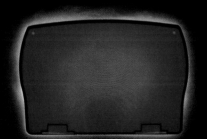

NOMAD CARPET
deep-pile woollen carpet with hidden mechanism for the adjustable 'back', 1998

LACE TABLE (Droog Design)
Swiss, fibreglass lace was hardened with resin to produce a transparent series of tables.
Their spun sugar character is very special and gives the products a crystalline appearance, 1997

Wanders Wonders is published in conjunction with an exibition of his work in
Het Kruithuis, Museum of Contemporary Art, in 's-Hertogenbosch,
The Netherlands.
The publication was made possible with the support of the Mondriaan Foundation
in Amsterdam.

Edited by Yvònne G.J.M. Joris
Texts by Paola Antonelli, curator of the Museum of Modern Art in New York;
Aaron Betsky, curator of the Museum of Modern Art in San Francisco;
Andrea Branzi, designer in Milano; Bart Lootsma, design critic, Rotterdam;
Renny Ramakers, director of Droog Design, Amsterdam and Marcel Wanders.
Marcel Wanders' texts were dictated to Inez van der Linden and edited
by Gert Staal.
Translations from the Dutch by Ted Alkins, Bertem
Design by Roelof Mulder, Amsterdam
Lithography by Lithopartners, Amsterdam
Printed by Snoeck Ducaju, Gent

ISBN 90-6450-376-1/010 Publishers, Rotterdam (www.010publishers.nl)

Thanks to Boffi, Cappellini, Disc & Partners, Van Engelen & Evers, Magis,
Triodos Bank, De Voogt Systemen.